COUNTRY

Formal Name: French Republic (République Française).

Short Form: France.

Term for Citizen(s): Frenchman/Frenchwoman. Adjective: French.

Capital: Paris.

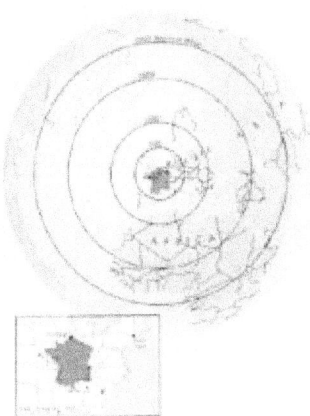

Click to Enlarge Image

Major Cities: The country's capital Paris, the only French city with more than 1 million inhabitants, has a population of 2,142,800 in the city proper (as of 2004) and 11,330,700 in the metropolitan area (2003 estimate). Greater metropolitan Paris encompasses more than 15 percent of the country's total population. The second largest city is Marseille, a major Mediterranean seaport, with about 795,600 inhabitants. Other major cities include Lyon, an industrial center in east-central France, with 468,300 inhabitants, and the second largest metropolitan area in France, with 1,665,700 people. Further important cities include: Toulouse, 426,700, a manufacturing and European aviation center in southwestern France; Nice, 339,000, a resort city on the French Riviera; Nantes, 276,200, a seaport and shipbuilding center on the Atlantic coast; Strasbourg, 273,100, the principal French port on the Rhine River and a seat of the European parliament (in addition to Brussels); Montpellier, 244,700, a commercial and manufacturing city in southern France; and Bordeaux, 229,500, a major seaport in southwestern France and the principal exporting center for key French vineyard regions. According to the 1999 decadal census, more than 25 additional French cities had populations surpassing 100,000.

Independence: July 14, Bastille Day, is France's national holiday.

Public Holidays: New Year's Day (January 1); Easter Monday (variable date in March or April); Labor Day (May 1); Ascension Day (Thursday, 40 days after Easter); World War II Victory Day (May 8); Bastille Day (July 14); Assumption (August 15); All Saints' Day (November 1); Armistice Day (November 11); and Christmas Day (December 25).

Flag: The French flag features three equal vertical bands of blue (on the hoist side), white, and red. Known as the "Le drapeau tricolore" (French Tricolor), the flag dates to 1790, in the era of the French Revolution.

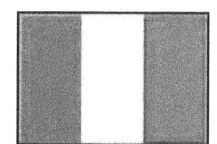

Click to Enlarge Image

HISTORICAL BACKGROUND

Pre-modern hominid populations migrated to France during Paleolithic times, and between 30,000 and 10,000 years ago, modern humans left evidence of their presence in cave art. After 600 B.C. Greek and Phoenician traders operated along the French Mediterranean coast, while Celts migrated westward from the Rhine valley, settling the territory later called Gaul by the Romans. The Romans under Julius Caesar conquered part of Gaul in 57–52 B.C., and it remained Roman until the Western Roman Empire disintegrated into small-scale agrarian settlements as the Franks invaded in the fifth century A.D. An interval of territorial consolidation occurred in the eighth century under the Frankish King Charlemagne, who took the title of Holy Roman Emperor. After his death, his three grandsons divided his empire among themselves and held territories corresponding roughly to France, Germany, and Italy. These territories became increasingly feudalized, with rule by numerous local lords. Vikings or "Northmen" raided coastal settlements, colonized Normandy, a territory named after them, and in 1066 conquered England, installing Duke William—William the Conqueror—as King of England. In the meantime, from 987 and for the next 350 years, an unbroken line of Capetian kings added to their domain, the region surrounding Paris known as the Île-de-France. As royal power gained ground against the feudal lords, the great monastic orders and emerging towns fueled an economic and cultural flowering. By 1328 and the accession of Philip VI, the first of the Valois kings, France boasted the highest achievements of medieval European culture—its Romanesque and Gothic architecture—and was the most powerful nation in Europe, with a population of 15 million. This population, like others in Europe, suffered a demographic disaster after 1348, when the Black Death (bubonic plague) entered France through Marseille and killed as many as one-third of the country's inhabitants.

A decade before the Black Death struck, disputed territorial and dynastic claims between France and England led to the Hundred Years' War (1337–1453) in France. When the French eventually won, with the help of the young Joan of Arc, the English retained no French possessions except Calais. The Valois dynasty's holdings came to resemble modern France, once Burgundy and Brittany were added. After the 1540s, the Protestantism of John Calvin spread throughout France and led to civil wars. The Edict of Nantes (1598), issued by Henry IV of the Bourbon dynasty, sustained Catholicism as the established religion of France but granted religious tolerance to the French Protestants (Huguenots) and calmed religious conflict. Absolute monarchy reached its apogee in the reign of Louis XIV (1643–1715), the Sun King, who built the Palace of Versailles, a celebration of French art and architecture.

The ambitious projects and military campaigns of Louis and his successors led to chronic financial problems in the eighteenth century. Deteriorating economic conditions and popular resentment against the system of privileges and tax exemptions enjoyed by the nobility and clergy were among the principal causes of the French Revolution (1789–94). The Revolution ended unchecked monarchical rule, enhanced the power of non-noble elites, and brought more equitable land distribution to the peasantry. French revolutionary ideals—especially ideals of nationhood and universal rights—long proved a powerful influence on the development of national movements elsewhere in the world. However, France's own first experiment in republican and egalitarian government fell into turmoil, culminating in the "Reign of Terror." France reverted to forms of dictatorship or constitutional monarchy on four occasions in the nineteenth century—the Empire of Napoléon Bonaparte (1804–14, and three-month restoration, 1815), the Bourbon Restoration (1814–30), the reign of Louis-Philippe (1830–48), and the Second Empire of Napoléon III (1852–70). Under Napoléon Bonaparte, France extended its rule and cultural influence over most of Europe before suffering defeat at Waterloo in 1815. Another defeat a half century later, in the Franco-Prussian War (1870), ended the rule of Napoléon III and ushered in the Third Republic, which lasted until France's military defeat at the hands of Nazi Germany in 1940. Throughout these changes in the political landscape, France remained among the world's leaders in industrialization, science and technology, and eventually labor and social legislation. France was also a major participant in Europe's colonial expansion, second only to Britain in the extent of its empire in Africa, the Middle East, and the Far East. Finally, France remained a magnet for generations of avant-garde artists and writers.

Although on the victorious side in World War I, France bore the brunt of the war's huge human and material losses and emerged at the end of 1918 determined to keep Germany weak through systems of alliances and defenses. Despite these, France was defeated by Nazi Germany early in World War II. In 1940 Nazi troops marched into an undefended Paris, and Marshal Henri Philippe Pétain signed an armistice. France was divided into an occupied north and an unoccupied south, Vichy France, which became a German puppet state with Pétain as its head. Vichy France acquiesced in the plunder of French resources and the deportation of forced labor and Jews to Germany. After four years, Allied armies liberated France in August 1944, and a provisional government was established, headed by General Charles de Gaulle, the wartime leader of Free France. In 1946 de Gaulle resigned, and a new constitution set up the Fourth Republic, featuring a parliamentary form of government controlled by a series of party coalitions. Under this governmental arrangement, France took important steps in promoting international cooperation, when it joined the North Atlantic Treaty Organization (NATO) and spearheaded European integration. In 1951, in a dramatic reconciliation, France and Germany, along with four other countries, founded the European Coal and Steel Community. It featured a joint administration, parliament, and supreme court, institutions that still govern today's European Union (EU). In 1957 France and the same five countries created a broader economic bloc, the European Economic Community, or Common Market, when they acceded to the Treaty of Rome, the core agreement of the EU.

Notwithstanding its accomplishments, the French government was prone to cabinet crises and proved inadequate to the challenge of the independence struggles of the country's colonies in French Indochina, or present-day Vietnam (1945–54), and Algeria (1954–62). France's war against communist insurgents in Indochina was abandoned after the defeat of French forces at Dien Bien Phu in 1954. A revolt in Algeria proved so divisive in France as to threaten a military coup there, prompting the National Assembly in 1958 to invite de Gaulle to return as premier with extraordinary powers. Under the new Gaullist constitution for a Fifth Republic, which strengthened the presidency and reduced legislative power, he was elected president in December 1958. Under de Gaulle, the dissolution of France's overseas empire continued. The French protectorates of Morocco and Tunisia had received independence in 1956. In 1960 French West Africa was partitioned, and the new nations were granted independence. Algeria, after a long civil war, finally became independent in 1962. Many of the former colonies maintained close economic and cultural ties with France.

In an example of France's occasionally maverick foreign policy, de Gaulle took France out of the NATO military command in 1967 and expelled all foreign-controlled troops from the country. De Gaulle's government was weakened by massive protests in May 1968 when student rallies merged with wildcat strikes by millions of factory workers across France. The movement aimed at transforming the authoritarian, elitist French system of governance and came close to forcing de Gaulle from power. After order was reestablished in 1969, de Gaulle resigned and his successor, Georges Pompidou (1969–74), modified Gaullist policies to include a stronger market orientation in domestic economic affairs. Valéry Giscard d'Estaing, elected president in 1974, also supported conservative, pro-business policies.

Socialist François Mitterrand was elected president in 1981, beginning a record 14-year tenure in that office. He saw seven prime ministers and two periods of "cohabitation" (1986–88 and 1993–95) in which the prime minister was from the center-right opposition. He also saw France's first female prime minister, Edith Cresson (1991–92). Early in the Mitterrand presidency, the victorious socialists, carrying out their campaign pledges, imposed a wealth tax, nationalized key industries, decreed a 39-hour workweek and five-week paid vacations, halted nuclear testing, suspended nuclear power plant construction, and abolished the death penalty. The most notable and lasting achievements of the Mitterrand presidency, however, came in the international arena, where France's major commitment remained the European Economic Community and, especially, improved Franco-German relations, regarded as the key to Europe's integration. Under Mitterrand, after decades of ups and downs, the Common Market got a boost from the 1986 Single European Act, which eased the free movement of goods and labor. A capstone accomplishment came in the 1992 Treaty of Maastricht, which established a common currency and created the EU to coordinate foreign policy and immigration as well as economics. In promoting the treaty and monetary union, Mitterrand worked well with Germany's Chancellor Helmut Kohl, strengthening Franco-German economic and security ties.

France continued to be a driving force behind the EU's progress and expansion under the center-right Gaullist Jacques Chirac, who won the presidency in 1995 on a platform of reducing France's chronically high unemployment. Chirac briefly resumed France's nuclear testing in the South Pacific, despite widespread international protests. During his five years of cohabitation (1997–2002) with a socialist legislative majority, the euro was introduced (2002) and the franc retired as legal tender. In 1999 France took part in the NATO airstrikes in Kosovo, despite some internal opposition. In the 2002 election season, Jean-Marie Le Pen, leader of the neo-fascist, anti-immigrant National Front party, shocked France with his strong performance, a second-place finish in the first round of voting. He took 17 percent of the vote, handing a humiliating defeat to Lionel Jospin, the Socialist prime minister, whose party threw its support behind the incumbent Chirac and bolstered his overwhelming victory of 82 percent in the runoff election.

In 2003, in Chirac's second term, France defied the United States and the United Kingdom in the run-up to the Iraq War by calling for more weapons inspections and diplomacy. France's stance, although backed by popular sentiment in France, severely strained relations with the United States. In the domestic arena, the Chirac government pressed for unpopular belt-tightening and regulatory reforms of, for example, the pension and wage systems, in order to meet the budgetary requirements for monetary union laid out in the Maastricht Treaty. Proposed reforms were greeted each time with protests and street demonstrations across France. Voters also gave Chirac a major setback in May 2005, when they rejected the EU constitution, which he had strongly backed. In November 2005, widespread riots in France's largely immigrant-origin suburbs expressed a diffuse dissatisfaction and elicited much soul-searching in France about the French approach to immigrant integration and social problems.

In 2007, in the two-round presidential election, Nicolas Sarkozy of the center-right party defeated Ségolène Royal, the Socialist candidate and France's would-be first female president, by a majority of 53 to 47 percent. Sarkozy has appointed fellow conservative and four-time minister François Fillon as prime minister and a cabinet of 15 ministers, including one to serve in a controversial new post of minister of immigration and national identity. Among Sarkozy's ministerial appointees are the popular Socialist Bernard Kouchner, founder of the Nobel Prize-winning organization Doctors Without Borders, and seven women, including a justice minister of North African descent. Parliamentary elections in June 2007 are expected to deliver a majority for the center-right party that Sarkozy leads.

GEOGRAPHY

Location: France is composed of its metropolitan territory located in Western Europe and a collection of overseas islands and territories located on other continents. The French often refer to metropolitan France as the "Hexagon" because of its shape. Three of the Hexagon's six sides are bounded by water—the English Channel and North Sea on the northwest, the Atlantic Ocean and Bay of Biscay on the west, and the Mediterranean Sea on the southeast. The remaining sides, mostly mountainous, abut Spain and Andorra in the southwest, Belgium and Luxembourg in the northeast, and Germany, Switzerland, and Italy in the east. The United Kingdom, to the northwest, is now linked to France via the Channel Tunnel, which passes underneath the English Channel.

Click to Enlarge Image

Size: The largest West European nation, France has a total area of 547,030 square kilometers (or somewhat smaller than California and New England combined). This area total includes the island of Corsica (8,721 square kilometers) and 1,400 square kilometers of water. Corsica, considered part of metropolitan France, is in the Mediterranean, about 185 kilometers east-southeast of Nice. France's area total excludes its 10 overseas possessions, mostly remnants of France's colonial empire. Referred to as "DOM–TOM"—for *domaines d'outre-mer* and *territoires d'outre-mer*—these possessions include several that are considered to be official departments of France: Guadeloupe and Martinique in the Caribbean, French Guiana in South America, and Réunion in the Indian Ocean. Of these, French Guiana, now used for France's space launches, is by far the largest, at 91,000 square kilometers.

Land Boundaries: France's land boundaries total 2,889 kilometers. France borders Belgium (620 kilometers) and Luxembourg (73 kilometers) to the northeast; Germany (451 kilometers), Switzerland (573 kilometers), and Italy (488 kilometers) to the east; and Spain (623 kilometers) and (Andorra 56.6 kilometers) to the southwest. Monaco is completely enclosed by France.

Length of Coastline: France has coastlines along the Atlantic Ocean, the English Channel, and the Mediterranean Sea. These total 3,427 kilometers, including Corsica's 644 kilometers of coastline.

Maritime Claims: France's territorial sea extends 12 nautical miles. The continental shelf extends to 200-meter depth or to the depth of exploitation, and the contiguous zone is 24 nautical miles. The exclusive economic (fishing) zone extends 200 nautical miles but does not apply to the Mediterranean. Because of France's far-flung maritime openings on the world's oceans, its exclusive economic zone ranks third in the world behind the United States and the United Kingdom.

Topography: France features mostly coastal lowlands, flat plains, and gently rolling hills in the north and west. South-central France has hilly uplands. Mountainous and hilly areas lie on nearly all of France's borders, creating a series of natural boundaries. Only the nation's northeastern border is largely exposed. The two principal mountain chains are the Pyrenees, which form the border with Spain, and the Alps, which form most of the border with Switzerland and Italy. The Pyrenees are a formidable barrier because of the absence of low passes and the chain's elevation—several summits exceed 3,000 meters. The French Alps, at the western end of the European Alpine chain, are also high, with elevations of 3,500 meters, but are broken by several important river valleys, including the Rhône, Isère, and Durance, providing access to Switzerland and Italy. The Jura range on the Swiss border is a lower and less rugged component of the Alpine chain. In the Alps near the Italian and Swiss borders is Western Europe's highest point—Mont Blanc, at 4,810 meters. The country's lowest point is the Rhône River delta, at two meters below sea level.

Principal Rivers: Several major rivers—extensively navigable—drain France, including the Seine, Loire, Garonne, and Rhône. Three of the streams flow west: the Seine into the English Channel; the Loire—France's longest river—into the Atlantic; and the Garonne into the Bay of Biscay. The Rhône—France's deepest river—flows south into the Mediterranean. For about 161 kilometers, the Rhine constitutes the southern part of the border between France and Germany.

Climate: France's climate is generally temperate and well suited to agriculture, with major variations: the oceanic and Mediterranean climates. The oceanic climate prevails throughout much of the country, especially in the north and west, where westerly winds from the Atlantic Ocean bring mild and moist conditions. These winds produce cool summers, mild winters with little snow and frost, and year-round rainfall, which usually falls as slow, steady drizzle. Paris, for example, receives 650 millimeters of precipitation annually, with rain occurring an average of 188 days each year. The average daily temperature range in Paris is 1°C to 6°C in January and 13°C to 24°C in July. The Mediterranean climate brings much warmer winters and hot, dry summers along the southern coast.

Natural Resources: France's most valuable natural asset is its rich agricultural land. High-quality soils cover almost half the country's surface, giving France an agricultural surplus that makes it an exporter of food. The country's varied physiography, with beaches, rivers, forests, and mountains, is a draw for the tourism industry. France is not well endowed with indigenous energy supplies or other mineral resources. Hydroelectric production, although well developed, is inadequate to France's needs.

Land Use: Of France's land surface, about 33.46 percent is arable and in annually replanted crops, while 2.03 percent is in permanent crops, such as fruit trees and vines. According to a 1998 estimate, an area of about 20,000 square kilometers was irrigated.

Environmental Factors: France faces the usual environmental degradation associated with industrial economies, including air pollution from industrial and vehicle emissions, water pollution from urban wastes and agricultural runoff, soil erosion, acid rain forest damage, and the loss and fragmentation of open space and wildlife habitat. To address these issues, France established the Ministry of the Environment in 1971 and undertook a variety of environmental protection initiatives.

A cornerstone of France's efforts is to preserve open space and species through the creation of a system of parks and nature reserves. Today, forests and woodlands cover nearly 30 percent of the country, and about 10 percent of the French national territory enjoys some type of protected status. This protected area includes six national parks, several dozen regional nature parks, and more than 100 smaller nature reserves. Successive French governments have also directed environmental efforts against pollution of the air and water. To control its air pollution problem, now mainly caused by transport emissions, the French Environment and Energy Control Agency has developed a monitoring system in accordance with the national Air Pollution Act. The government promotes energy efficiency and emissions reduction with measures to encourage the use of public transportation and cleaner fuels.

Because of such efforts, as well as reliance on nuclear power for most electricity generation, France is closer than other countries to meeting its pledged greenhouse gas emission targets under the 1997 Kyoto Protocol. France's per capita carbon emissions are already the lowest among the major West European countries and declining. Since 1980 the country has cut its energy-related carbon emissions by about 20 percent to 108 million metric tons (2001), somewhat short of its Kyoto target of 102 million metric tons. By 2001 the per capita emissions had declined to 1.83 metric tons of carbon equivalent. In comparison, per capita emissions in 2001 in other large European Union (EU) countries ranged from 2.71 metric tons of carbon equivalent in Germany to 2.05 metric tons in Spain. In 1999 U.S. emissions averaged more than 5 metric tons of carbon per head. In 2000 the French government's Inter-Ministerial Greenhouse Effect Mission unveiled a 96-point plan for further carbon emission reductions in the 2000–10 period. French measures include a gradually rising carbon tax, which is linked to the 1999 General Tax on Polluting Activities, an ecology tax that will be extended to energy consumption by businesses and electricity producers.

France is also a leader in efforts to prevent marine pollution. As the victim of major oil tanker spills in 1999 and 2002, which were disastrous for the tourism and fishing industries along France's Atlantic seaboard, France spearheaded more stringent EU regulations on tankers and set in motion constitutional changes in France that would hold polluters financially responsible for damages to fishing, beaches, and wildlife. France, with the support of neighboring countries, also extended its jurisdiction in the Mediterranean from 19 to 145 kilometers, reserving the right to sentence captains of large polluting vessels to fines of up to US$600,000 or four years in prison.

Time Zone: France lies in one time zone, which is one hour ahead of Greenwich Mean Time (GMT+1). The country observes daylight saving time.

SOCIETY

Population: In 2006 the population of France was estimated at 60,876,136, up by more than 2 million since the last census in 1999. In addition, 1.9 million live in France's overseas departments and territories. The annual population growth rate has averaged about 0.4 percent in recent years, less than half the U.S. rate but somewhat above the low West European norm. Nearly all of the European Union (EU) population growth in recent years has come from France, as in 2003, when France added 211,000 out of the EU's 216,000 total increase. The population density in France proper is 111 people per square kilometer of land area (2005 estimate). Three-quarters of the French population live in urban settings, defined as cities and towns with more than 2,000 inhabitants.

Demography: Since the late eighteenth century, France's demographic pattern has differed from that of other West European countries. France was the most populous country in Europe until 1795 and the third most populous in the world, behind only China and India. However, unlike the rest of Europe, France did not experience strong population growth in the nineteenth century and first half of the twentieth century. The country's birthrate dropped after the French Revolution, when the peasantry gained an ownership stake in land and then limited births to ensure passing on viable plots of land to their children. Thanks to this limitation, France effected the "demographic transition" to lower birthrates much earlier than other countries, and France's population eventually fell in comparative terms behind Germany, the United Kingdom, and Italy, as well as a score of non-West European countries. After World War II, France was again atypical among European countries, in that its postwar baby boom lasted longer than elsewhere. As a result, since 1991 France has regained its position behind only Germany as the most populous West European nation. If present trends continue, the French will outnumber the Germans by mid-century.

Estimates on current total fertility rates in France range from very slightly above to slightly below the replacement level of 2.1 births per woman. Women continue to postpone childbearing through high contraception usage (legalized in 1967) and abortion (legalized in 1974). In 2004 the average age of women who gave birth was 29.6. Notwithstanding this late childbearing, the native birthrate has been rising slightly and stands at 11.99 per 1,000 (2006 estimate). Infant mortality stands at an extremely low level, 4.2 deaths per 1,000 live births in 2006. The overall death rate is 9.14 deaths per 1,000 population (2006 estimate).

The most striking demographic feature of France, as of other advanced industrial countries, is population aging. France's median age is 39.1 years. Life expectancy for men and women combined stood at 79.7 in 2006, with men living 76.1 years and women living 83.5 years. Life expectancy gains stem from reductions in adult mortality, with more and more of all deaths occurring in advanced old age. The age structure of the population is typical for Europe, with 18.3 percent under 15 and 16.4 percent over 65, a number expected to grow to 24 percent in 2030. If labor market behavior remains unchanged, France's labor force will begin to shrink and age significantly after 2010. One person in four of working age will be over 50 in 2010, compared with one in five at the present time.

Positive net migration—0.66 migrants per 1,000 in 2006—plays a relatively minor role in France's population dynamics, and, once immigrants are settled in the country, their birthrates fall rather quickly toward the local norm. According to French statistics, this change can occur within a single generation.

Ethnic Groups and Languages: The national language is French. Some rapidly declining regional dialects and languages also are spoken, including Alsatian, Basque, Breton, Catalan, Corsican, Flemish, and Provençal. French derived from the vernacular Latin spoken by the Romans in Gaul. Historically, French served as the international language of diplomacy, and it remains a unifying force in parts of the world, chiefly, Africa.

France is the most ethnically diverse country of Europe. A crossroads since prehistoric times, the country's "historic populations" were a blend of European ethnic stocks, Celtic (Gallic and Breton), Aquitanian (related to Basque), Latin, and Germanic. Over the past 200 years, France has been unusual among European states in periodically attracting large-scale immigration. In the nineteenth century, the new populations that arrived—forebears of 40 percent of today's inhabitants—included southern Europeans, Belgians, Poles, Armenians, East European and Maghrebi Jews, Maghrebi Arabs and Berbers, sub-Saharan Africans, and Chinese. After World War II, large-scale immigration to France initially came mainly from southern Europe and subsequently from France's former colonial possessions, especially North Africa. Other ethnic minorities from the French colonial empire—apart from North African Muslims—are the Indochinese and francophone sub-Saharan Africans.

Among European countries, France has the largest number of people of Muslim origin, perhaps 5–6 million, although some estimate only 2.6 million. The exact number of Muslims of different national origins living in France is not known, because the state does not collect religious or ethnic census data. The Muslim presence in France is of an earlier date than Muslim communities in Germany and the United Kingdom. More than 1 million Muslims immigrated in the 1960s and early 1970s from North Africa, especially Algeria.

France's last census figures—for 1999—showed 4.33 million foreign nationals living in France, and every year a further 140,000 enter using legal channels, overwhelmingly family reunification. In addition, some 90,000 are believed to enter illegally every year, mainly by overstaying on short-term visas. The government believes there are between 200,000 and 400,000 "*sans-papiers*"—literally, "paperless ones." Resisting calls to regularize their situation, the government has recently toughened its stance on immigration, for example, increasing the number of deportations, as well as the number of people refused asylum. In 2006 the government expects to make 26,000 repatriations.

Religion: Between 83 percent and 90 percent of the French population is Roman Catholic and only 2 percent Protestant. The rate of religious practice among the nominally Catholic population is very low. France also has a Jewish minority of about 1 percent, a Muslim minority of 5–10 percent, and about 4 percent unaffiliated. France's Muslim population is the largest in Europe.

France lacks official statistics on religion, a fact that reflects the country's commitment to the religious neutrality of the state, or *laïcité*, considered necessary for religious freedom. Faced with antidemocratic pressures from the Catholic Church in the early decades of the Third Republic, France promulgated a law in 1905 calling for the strict separation of church and state. The government has since reaffirmed this law, with, for example, a controversial March 2004 bill that banned the display of all conspicuous religious symbols in public schools. This ban targeted in particular the wearing of headscarves by Muslim girls in public schools. The government maintains that the wearing of religious symbols threatens the country's secular identity, while others contend that the ban on symbols curtails religious freedom.

France currently seeks to encourage the emergence of a "French Islam." In 2002 the government set up the French Council for the Islamic Faith based on the model of the Consistoire for Jews created in 1808. The government also has called on private divinity schools to train tolerant homegrown imams who can compete with more militant foreign imams. At present, fewer than 20 percent of France's approximately 1,600 imams have French citizenship, only a third speak French with ease, and half of those who receive regular pay receive it from foreign sources, mainly Algerian, Moroccan, Turkish, and Saudi. Many imams work in unknown "backyard mosques," a concern for both security agencies and Muslim leaders.

Education and Literacy: France's literacy rate is 99 percent. The highly centralized state education system is free between ages two and 18 and compulsory for both citizens and non-citizens between ages six and 16. Free preschool and kindergarten for children under age six is widely available. During the school year 2001–2, the percentage of children attending school was 100 percent for ages three to 13, dropping off slightly for ages 14 to 16. Most children in France continue in education beyond age 16. Top students go to high school (lycée) to study for the baccalaureat qualification, while others attend vocational school. Outside the public education system, private education, primarily Roman Catholic, is also available, involving about 20 percent of French pupils.

Every high-school graduate who passes the baccalaureat exam is guaranteed a free—or nearly free—university education. Higher education in France, which began with the founding of the University of Paris in 1150, now consists of 91 public universities and 175 professional schools, such as the postgraduate Grandes Ecoles, the most competitive and prestigious French universities; technical colleges; and vocational training institutions. University enrollment is high, but only 4 percent of French students make it into the Grandes Ecoles. French higher education, apart from the Grandes Ecoles, is widely considered under-resourced, given the system's growing enrollments. In 2005 about 25 percent of 21–24 year olds were participating in higher education. About 19 percent complete postsecondary education (by age 34).

Health: The health status of the French population, as reflected in health and mortality indicators, ranks among the best in the industrialized countries. French life expectancy increases more than three months each year, and female life expectancy at birth (83.5 years) was second in the world after Japan in 2006. Male life expectancy, at 76.1, is unsatisfactorily low, largely because of excess road accidents and suicide. Infant mortality is just above the very low levels in Scandinavian countries.

As in other developed countries, the principal causes of death are the major noncommunicable diseases such as cardiovascular disease (31.1 percent of deaths) and cancer (27.7 percent). Other top causes are accidents (8.3 percent) and diseases of the respiratory system (8.1 percent). In 2005 France reported an adult human immunodeficiency virus (HIV) prevalence rate of 0.4 percent and 130,000 people living with HIV. From the beginning of the epidemic through June 2005, authorities reported 60,212 acquired immune deficiency syndrome (AIDS) cases and 34,351 AIDS deaths.

The general health of the French population reflects in part the success of the French health system. In 2000 the World Health Organization (WHO) issued a first ever—predictably contentious—comparative analysis of 191 of the world's health systems. The WHO ranked the French health care system as the "best health system in the world" (while the U.S. system was ranked 37). The WHO's assessment was based on five performance indicators: overall level of population health; social disparities in care; health system responsiveness (measured partly by patient satisfaction); distribution of service within the population; and distribution of the health system's financial burden, including out-of-pocket expenses.

France's total expenditure on health as a percentage of gross domestic product (GDP) is 10.1, among the highest rates in the Organisation for Economic Co-operation and Development (OECD) but significantly lower than the U.S. rate of 16 percent. French spending is higher than other universal systems, such as that of the United Kingdom, which spends an unusually low 6 percent of GDP. France's per capita expenditure is about US$2,902 (2003).

The French system is a national health insurance (NHI) system, with a public-private mix of hospital and ambulatory care. It provides universal coverage and comprehensive benefits, with the right to health insurance coverage on the basis of residence in France. Providers such as doctors and dentists are free to establish private practices. Patients are free to choose their own providers, usually require no referrals to see specialists, and generally encounter no significant waiting lists for treatment. Health spending is reimbursed generously by the state. At the same time, private insurers are not excluded from the supplementary insurance market. Low-income people receive extra help with their health spending. Given the strengths of the system—quality of care, freedom of choice, and equity of access, the French population is relatively satisfied with the health system. However, the recognized strengths come at the price of high and rising costs. Reform efforts to rein in costs, which have shifted costs to the patient through higher out-of-pocket payments, have proven ineffective and raise equity questions.

Welfare: France is among the most successful major countries in limiting disparities of income and wealth and in containing poverty. To use a summary measure of inequality, the Gini coefficient, which ranges from 0 (perfect equality) to 1 (perfect inequality), France reduced inequality over the past quarter century to 0.248 (2004), below the average of the Organisation for Economic Co-operation and Development and significantly below the United States, which

11

has seen large increases, to 0.450. French households in the lowest tenth of the income distribution receive about 54 percent of the income of the median household (the household in the middle of the income distribution), compared to 39 percent in the United States. France's top-decile income share has held steady over the past 20 years, while that of the United States has risen dramatically.

One factor contributing to France's relative containment of inequality is a high minimum wage, twice that of the United States. Another factor is the country's generosity in its provision of many forms of social protection, apart from universal health insurance. In 2003 France's expenditure on social protection and fringe benefits was 30.9 percent of gross domestic product, somewhat above the Eurozone average of 28.1 percent. The major components of what France calls the national social security system—"Sécurité Sociale" or Sécu—are old-age pensions, health insurance, disability income and worker's compensation, family allocations, unemployment insurance, survivor benefits, and housing subsidies. A typical low-income working family of four can receive more than US$1,200 a month in various benefits and transfers. The elderly receive the bulk of benefits. Old-age pensions and health care for the elderly consume 70 percent of the budget for social spending.

Because the population is aging, France faces strong financial pressure to reduce benefits and increase contributions to the Sécu system. In adjusting the system, the general proposed direction is to increase means-testing for benefits and to pay for a greater share out of tax revenues rather than compulsory employer- and employee-paid social insurance. Currently, Sécu is funded mainly by a tax on jobs, which is split, unevenly, between workers and employers. People on average salaries, even including the Sécu tax, pay a relatively modest amount in personal taxes in France: 29 percent, compared with 26.5 percent in the United Kingdom (UK). The great burden of Sécu falls on employers. French companies, large and small, pay the equivalent of 42.3 percent in tax on top of each salary—compared with 10.5 percent in the UK.

ECONOMY

Overview: With a gross domestic product (GDP) in 2006 of US$2,124 billion, France is the sixth largest economy in the world in U.S. dollar terms, after the United States, Japan, Germany, the People's Republic of China, and the United Kingdom (UK). France is a member of the European Union and, as part of the Eurozone, has ceded its monetary policy authority to the European Central Bank in Frankfurt. For the past two decades, the French economy has undergone substantial adjustments that diminished public ownership and economic planning and increased the sway of markets, especially financial markets, over French business. At its high-water mark in 1985, public ownership accounted for 10 percent of the economy and public-sector employment for 10 percent of employment. By 2000, public-sector employment had been cut in half, and the state's direct control of the economy was reduced to core areas of public-service provision, such as the post office.

Currently, the French economy is performing strongly by several measures of economic activity. In 2005 productivity measured as GDP per hour worked exceeded that of the United States and the other Group of Eight economies. Large French companies are expanding internationally and performing impressively in the global arena of economics and trade. And France has comparatively low inequality and the lowest poverty rate among the world's large economies, at 7 percent, compared to 15 percent in the UK and 18 percent in the United States. At the same time, the country is struggling to reconcile its commitment to social equity with the demands of more open European and global markets. The most troubling aspect of the economy is persistently high unemployment—between 8 and 10 percent—and underemployment. Companies faced with stepped-up international competition have tended to substitute capital for France's comparatively costly labor. Job creation has failed to keep pace with the number of jobs lost to enterprise downsizing, and many jobs created in the services sector, the most dynamic sector, are inferior to previously available unskilled and semi-skilled jobs. The result in France, as elsewhere, is an economy of insiders and long-term outsiders, where some enjoy secure, well-paid jobs with benefits, while others—mostly youth, especially youth of immigrant descent—are saddled with insecure, poorly paid work with reduced and diminishing benefits.

Gross Domestic Product (GDP): France's GDP is substantially smaller than that of the United States, Japan, Germany, and China, and slightly smaller than that of the United Kingdom (UK). In 2006 France's GDP was about US$2,124 billion. Per capita GDP was US$33,894, about the average level in the Organisation for Economic Co-operation and Development (OECD) and about 30 percent lower than in the United States. Most of the difference between French and U.S. per capita GDP results from fewer hours worked in France per employed person. France also has an employment rate—share of the working-age population employed—somewhat below the OECD average. Overall, French workers contribute fewer hours to GDP than workers in most other OECD countries, and the higher hourly productivity of French workers only partially offsets the country's lower level of labor utilization. With shorter workweeks, longer vacations, earlier retirement, later youth employment, and higher unemployment, French workers work 40 to 41 weeks a year, about six weeks fewer than U.S. workers. Debate and research continue on whether differences in hours worked mainly reflect a greater preference for leisure in France or institutional labor or financial market disincentives to higher employment and job creation.

The country's average real GDP growth in recent years, like that of other continental economies, has been relatively lackluster. In 2006 French growth was 2.2 percent, up from 1.7 percent in 2005 but down from 2.3 percent in 2004, a year in which growth in the UK was 3.1 percent. French growth in 2006 placed the country's growth rate tenth among the 12 countries in the Eurozone. In 2007 a first-quarter acceleration in France's growth prompted forecasters to raise their projections to a growth rate of 2.4 percent for the year. The origins of France's GDP by sector in 2006 were as follows: agriculture, 2.5 percent; industry and mining, 22 percent; and services, 75 percent (including government services at about 20 percent of GDP).

Government Budget: France's 2005 revenues totaled US$1,060 billion, while its expenditures totaled US$1,144 billion, including capital expenditures of US$23 billion. The French budget for 2005 lowered the country's deficit to 2.9 percent of gross domestic product (GDP), bringing it for the first time in four years back under the Treaty on European Union (Maastricht Treaty) cap of 3 percent. In 2006 the deficit fell further to 2.5 percent of GDP. Public debt, the accumulation of past deficits, fell sharply from 66.2 percent in 2005 to 63.9 percent in 2006, somewhat below the U.S. level of about 65 percent of GDP (2005 to 2007), but still above the EU ceiling of 60.0 percent. Forecasts project further reductions in France's debt for 2007 and 2008. France is also expected to sustain a deficit well below 3 percent beyond 2006—possibly 2.3 percent in 2007—because of the pick-up in the economy's rate of GDP expansion. The pick-up is expected to generate tax receipts that offset health care cost increases (which a 2004 reform slowed but did not halt). In January 2007, because France's deficit had remained below 3 percent since 2005, the EU dropped a pending disciplinary action against France for running deficits above the 3 percent ceiling.

Inflation: In 2006 the inflation rate was 1.8 percent, slightly down from 1.9 percent in 2005, a year that also saw a rise in consumer spending of 2.4 percent. Lower international oil prices since mid-2006 have allowed inflation to remain below the European Central Bank's ceiling of 2 percent.

Agriculture, Forestry, and Fishing: Endowed with a third of all the agricultural land in the European Union (EU) and a moderate and varied climate, France is the world's second largest agricultural producer (behind the United States) and the EU's leading producer. French agricultural production makes up a fourth of the EU total and accounts for 2.5 percent of French gross domestic product (2006 estimate). France has roughly 1 million farms, which benefit substantially from subsidies, especially EU subsidies. Wheat, corn, meat, wine, sugar beets, and dairy products are France's main agricultural products.

The EU receives 70 percent of France's agricultural exports. French agricultural exports to the United States, mainly cheese, processed products, and wine, amount to about US$1.75 billion (2003) annually. The United States is the second-largest agricultural exporter to France, with exports—largely feeds, seafood, and snack foods—totaling US$425 million in 2003.

Several issues related to French agriculture figure in ongoing international debates. One issue is the magnitude of the subsidies that French agriculture receives under the EU's Common Agricultural Policy. Some EU states, such as Germany, consider the subsidies disproportionate and an unfair burden on their own resources, while other states, notably the United States, see them as a violation of free trade. Other issues involve France's insistence on the protection and security of its food supply. France's food security concerns prompt it to prefer food self-sufficiency (even at the cost of needing subsidies) and to close its doors to products that could pose a threat, such as genetically engineered foods.

France also has forest resources that are among the largest in Europe. The forests—about two-thirds deciduous—cover almost 17 million hectares and account for a third of the country's land area. The average figure per capita is 0.3 hectares. Forest cover is growing by about 30,000 hectares, or 0.4 percent a year, through encroachment on former agricultural land. This expansion of forested land partly reflects the continuation of long-existing forest expansion and improvement policies. Since 1947, the government has subsidized the reforestation of 2.1 million hectares of forestland, for a growth of forestland by 35 percent. A quarter of the country's forests are publicly owned, and 95 percent have free public access. State subsidies, amounting to some 90 million euros per year for the period 2000–9, have been earmarked for assisting communities and private owners to clear and regenerate their forests.

France's large and growing forestry and wood products sector employs about a quarter of a million people (2000) in some 35,000 companies. The country, which harvests 55 million cubic meters of timber annually, is the largest European producer of hardwood sawnwood and is self-sufficient in hardwood raw materials. It is a net importer of softwood sawnwood and pulp for the paper industry. At least half of the pulp consumed in France is recycled material. Trade in forestry products in 2001 amounted to US$2.4 billion in imports and US$1.9 billion in exports.

With maritime openings on all the planet's oceans, France has the world's third largest exclusive economic zone, behind the United States and the United Kingdom. In spite of this privileged access to large fishing zones, the northeast Atlantic Ocean remains the fishing zone of most of the French fishing fleet. The production of the French fishing industry is currently growing. In 2006 the catch was as follows: shellfish, mollusks, and cephalopods, 285,291 metric tons, and saltwater fish, 472,914 metric tons. Aquaculture production reached 793,413 metric tons in 2006.

Mining and Minerals: France is not especially rich in natural mineral resources, although the coal deposits of northern France and the iron ore deposits in the east were important in the nation's early industrialization. The country's limited iron ore is of poor quality, and the nearly depleted coal reserves are unsuitable for steel production. In 2004 coal mining in France by its state-owned company was phased out altogether in favor of limited imports. Deposits of petroleum and natural gas, small and largely tapped, each yield only 5 percent of France's consumption. France currently imports iron ore along with most other minerals important in industrial production. France remains a significant producer of uranium, a fuel used in nuclear reactors, and bauxite, from which aluminum is made.

Industry and Manufacturing: France has a large industrial base whose contribution to the country's economic activity has not diminished in favor of services as dramatically as in other developed countries. French industry still provides 22 percent of jobs, compared to 11 percent in the United States. French industry is highly diversified. Apart from agri-food processing, the key industrial sectors are chemicals and pharmaceuticals, automobiles, metallurgy, telecommunications and electronics, and aircraft. France has been particularly successful in developing dynamic telecommunications, aerospace, and weapons sectors. Toulouse is now Europe's aviation center.

Energy: France's total energy consumption in 2001 was 10.5 quadrillion British thermal units (Btu's), somewhat up compared to a decade previously. The country's per capita energy consumption—178 million Btu's in 2001—is slightly higher than in other West European countries but only about half the level of the United States (342 million Btu's per capita energy consumption).

Petroleum and nuclear power account for roughly equal fuel shares of France's total energy consumption—at 38 percent and 37 percent of consumption, respectively. With virtually no domestic oil production, France has relied heavily on the development of nuclear power, which now accounts for about 80 percent of the country's electricity production. The non-petroleum and non-nuclear 25 percent of French energy consumption is divided among natural gas (14 percent), coal (4 percent), and renewables, including hydroelectric (7 percent) and combined geothermal, solar, and wind power (less than 1 percent). France is far behind other European

Union (EU) countries, for example, Germany, in meeting the EU target of 20 percent renewable energy by 2010.

France is a net energy importer, with oil imports, chiefly from Saudi Arabia and Norway, accounting for most of the difference between the country's energy consumption and production. Although France uses only half as much oil per capita as the United States, France is the world's fifth-greatest net oil importer (behind the United States, Japan, Germany, and South Korea). France also imports more than 95 percent of its natural gas supply, mostly by pipeline from Norway, Russia, Algeria, and the Netherlands. France imports coal for its declining consumption from Australia, the United States, and South Africa.

The French economy was badly shaken by the oil shocks of the early 1970s, being overwhelmingly dependent on imported petroleum supplies. To reduce this dependence, France undertook both energy conservation measures and a crash program to develop its nuclear power industry. France now has more than one-sixth of the world's total nuclear-based electricity generating capacity, which ranks second in the world (behind the United States). France generates significantly more electricity than it consumes each year and exports the surplus to neighboring countries, mainly to Switzerland, the United Kingdom, Italy, and Germany.

Thanks to both moderate per person energy usage and heavy investment in the nuclear alternative, France is the most energy independent Western country. It is also the smallest producer of carbon dioxide among the world's seven most industrialized countries. France, however, faces a challenge in maintaining its current position, because its nuclear power has weakening public support for both environmental and economic reasons. Environmentalists are concerned about the possibility of accidents and about nuclear waste, which is currently stored on-site at reprocessing facilities. Nuclear power may also prove economically unattractive under new EU guidelines, which call for EU-wide competition in electricity markets. Nuclear power in France has hitherto been shielded from such competition, because for many years the state-owned Electricité de France (EdF) supplied electricity in France. The French government is now partially privatizing EdF.

Services: France's dynamic services sector accounts for an increasingly large share of economic activity (75 percent of gross domestic product in 2006) and has been responsible for nearly all job creation in recent years. The services sector is dominated by financial services, insurance, and tourism.

The banking system, which accounts for 3 percent of GDP, is the third largest private-sector employer in France, with about 500,000 employees. The system has recently seen rapid change through numerous mergers and acquisitions. These gave rise in 2000 to PNB Paribas, which became the largest bank in France and the second largest in the Eurozone in terms of market capitalization. Crédit Agricole ranks second in profits among the top 25 West European banks. Other French banks with global prominence include the recently expanded Société Générale and the recently privatized Crédit Lyonnais. The French insurance sector, which provides nearly 200,000 jobs, was the fifth largest in the world in 2003 and growing, particularly in the life, health, and property insurance classes.

The tourism sector, another major contributor to the French economy, generates 900,000 jobs and a trade surplus of well over US$10 billion yearly. France is the number-one tourist destination in the world, receiving more than 75 million tourists in 2005. The country has more than 17 million tourist beds, including more than 1 million in 40,000 hotels and 16 million in rural lodging, campsites, and youth hostels.

Labor: In 2005 about 28 million people were active in the labor force, for a labor market participation rate about 2 percent below the Organisation for Economic Co-operation and Development (OECD) average. Between 2000 and 2005, French employment growth averaged 3.1 percent (compared to 3.5 percent in the United States). The employment rate for male workers aged 25 to 54 is 87.6 percent (compared to 87.3 percent in the United States), but workers in France join the workforce later and retire earlier than workers in many other OECD countries. French workers also work relatively few hours yearly, averaging 37 hours per week (somewhat more than the statutory standard of 35 hours per week) with a statutory minimum of five weeks of paid vacation. At the same time, the worker productivity level measured by output per hour is among the world's highest, exceeding the U.S. level.

Except for Scandinavia, France has the world's highest female labor market participation rate, with women representing about 47 percent of the country's workforce. This rate, dramatically up over recent decades, reflects in part the structural increase in services-sector employment, which is heavily female, and in part the relative family-friendliness of French workplaces. In the past 20 years, the structure of French employment has shifted toward the services sector—now involving more than 70 percent of the workforce—away from manufacturing and construction, with about 22 percent, down from 38 percent in 1970. Workers in France receive help in balancing work and family through not only short worktime policies, but also generous subsidies for child care and preschool, sizable child benefits, and up to 26 weeks of paid parental leave, potentially followed by unpaid leave without job forfeiture. Preschool teachers have the equivalent of graduate training in early education and earn wages that are above the average for all employed women. In order to spend an equivalent amount to what France now invests in its family-leave policies and child-care provisions, the United States would have to spend between 1 percent and 1.5 percent of gross domestic product, or about US$115 billion to US$175 billion per year.

The labor code sets minimum standards for working conditions, e.g., the workweek (35 hours, with exceptions increasingly allowed), layoffs, overtime, and vacation. The code mandates the prorating of benefits between full-time and part-time work. A combination of regulation and collectively bargained agreements gives French workers robust employment protection. Although labor union membership in the private sector is lower than the low U.S. rate, French unions are capable of exerting pressure in political quarters by threatening strikes or resorting to the French tradition of mass mobilization.

France's employment protection legislation has not prevented the adjustment of private-sector French enterprises to their growing exposure to global market competition. French businesses have moved rapidly to streamline their workforces through downsizing and to raise worker productivity through up-skilling and increased capital intensity. The adjustment process, however, has resulted in inadequate job opportunities, particularly for youth. In the last 20 years, the country's unemployment rate—8.3 percent in 2007—has consistently exceeded 8 percent, hovering around the 10 percent threshold for more than a third of that time. The unemployment and underemployment problem is often blamed on France's robust labor regulation and high minimum wages, which are said to inhibit job creation and to price low-paid workers out of jobs. No consensus exists, however, on the cause of the problem. Recent OECD studies dispute the over-regulation explanation, noting that France does not differ significantly in the stringency of its labor protection legislation from low unemployment countries such as Austria (2.4 percent), the Netherlands (3.1 percent), Norway (2.3 percent) and Sweden (2.9 percent). Nonetheless, in March 2005 the French government, responding to business groups, passed legislation to give businesses somewhat more flexibility to negotiate overtime pay, vacation times, and workweeks that exceed the 35-hour statutory limit.

Foreign Economic Relations: France was the main driving force behind the economic integration of Europe and remains a powerful force in the European Union (EU). As the member states of Europe's institutions have grown in number, first to 15 and now to 25, the influence of France has necessarily diminished somewhat. Still, France's contribution to the EU budget, to directing personnel in the EU, and to shaping the EU's future is matched or exceeded only by Germany's. Although the rejection of the EU constitution by the French electorate in 2005 produced some consternation about continuing progress in European integration, the EU's constitutional basis and France's central place in the EU remain secure.

Apart from the EU, France plays a major role in many other international economic bodies and regional blocs, including all of the central formal and informal organizations of the industrialized countries, e.g., the Organisation for Economic Co-operation and Development (OECD) and the Group of Eight (G8) and numerous regional trade blocs and customs unions in areas where France was formerly active as a colonial power. France, for instance, is a member or plays an advisory role in African economic blocs and organizations, such as the African Development Bank and the Central African States Development Bank. France is one of the world's most important donors of development aid and loans, whether on a bilateral basis or through multinational agencies, such as the European Development Fund, the World Bank, and the International Monetary Fund.

Imports and Exports: The French economy is very open to foreign trade. Total trade—imports plus exports of goods and services—amounts to about 50 percent of gross domestic product in France. France is the second-largest trading nation in Western Europe (after Germany).

France, the world's fourth largest exporter of goods and the third largest exporter of services, sends 70 percent of its trade to European Union partners. Its main customers are Germany, Italy, the United Kingdom, Belgium, and Spain, along with the United States. In 2005 France's top-three export destinations were Germany (14.7 percent), Spain (9.6 percent), and Italy (8.7 percent), with the United States receiving 7.2 percent. In 2005 France's top-three import sources were Germany (18.9 percent), Belgium (10.7 percent), and Italy (8.2 percent), with the United States contributing 5.1 percent. France's chief exports are machinery and transportation equipment, chemicals, iron and steel products, agricultural products, and textiles and clothing. The chief imports are crude oil, machinery and equipment, chemicals, and agricultural products.

Trade Balance: In 2004, after achieving a positive foreign trade balance for goods for most of the previous decade, France saw a trade deficit, as the euro's strength damaged trade competitiveness and oil prices surged. Although exports grew in that year, imports grew faster. By 2005, the trade deficit had grown several-fold. In 2005 the value of goods imports reached US$473.3 billion, while exports came to only US$443.4 billion, yielding a negative trade balance of US$29.9 billion or about 1.4 percent of gross domestic product (compared to the U.S trade deficit of 5.8 percent in the same year).

Balance of Payments: France's current account, a broad measure that summarizes the flow of goods, services, income, and transfer payments into and out of the country, fell from surplus into deficit between 2003 and 2004, largely because of deterioration in the merchandise trade balance. Another factor negatively affecting France's balance of payments for several years has been a lower surplus on services, which has not been fully offset by a larger surplus on investment income. In addition, as usual, France posted a large deficit on transfers, reflecting its net contribution to the European Union budget and its contribution to international aid. Taken together, in 2005 all of the international interactions yielded a current account deficit of US$38.8 billion, or 1.8 percent of gross domestic product. The deficit more than quadrupled that of 2004. In 2006 the deficit was 1.9 percent of gross domestic product (compared to the 2006 U.S. deficit of 6.4 percent of GDP).

Foreign Investment: France is among the world's top destinations for investment by foreigners, whether portfolio investment or foreign direct investment. The formal French investment regime is now among the least restrictive in the world, with no generalized screening of investment by non-French entities. Restrictions on foreign investment in France gradually disappeared in the 1990s. In the 1980s, most acquisitions of a French company by foreign interests were subject to prior approval by the French Ministry of Economy. Since then rules on investment have been liberalized, first for investments by European Union (EU) companies, then for all foreign investments. Only investments involving public security, health, or defense interests are screened. Negative decisions are subject to appeal if they violate the EU treaty article that guarantees free movement of capital.

Foreigners now hold about 35 percent of the capital of publicly traded French companies. Numerous opportunities for investors, including foreign investors, have been opened up by France's ongoing privatization process, notwithstanding that privatization legislation gives the French government the option to maintain a "golden share" to "protect national interests." Foreign-controlled firms play a significant role in France's economy. They account for 22 percent of the workforce, 27 percent of capital expenditures, 30 percent of exports, and 30 percent of production. Europe is by far the main source of direct investment in France, while the United States is the most active single investor. About 2,000 affiliates of U.S firms are established in France, with about 540,000 jobs resulting from U.S.-origin investments.

A decade of reforms has not entirely overcome the traditional preference for national control of businesses and aversion to foreign investment in the French economy, especially non-EU investment. Labor organizations, for example, sometimes oppose acquisition of French businesses by U.S. firms, on the grounds that U.S. firms focus on short-term profits at the expense of employment and employees. Nonetheless, the French government is committed to providing national treatment to all foreign companies. It provides, for example, equal access to research and development (R&D) subsidies. In 2003 France ranked fourth among Organisation for Economic Co-operation and Development countries for research, after Japan, Germany, and the United States, with R&D expenditure of about 2.5 percent of gross domestic product. More than half was financed by the public sector, which operates the major national research centers, as well as numerous centers specialized in particular fields.

Currency and Exchange Rate: As part of the Eurozone, France uses the euro as its unit of currency, having relinquished the franc as legal tender in 2002. The value of the euro has been rising in relation to the dollar. In late May 2007, the exchange rate was 0.74 euros=US$1.

Fiscal Year: France's fiscal year is the calendar year.

TRANSPORTATION AND TELECOMMUNICATIONS

Overview: France has a high-quality transport infrastructure in which road, rail, air, and water transport all play a significant role. The land transport infrastructure is among the best in the world and continues to improve. The closing decades of the twentieth century saw the development of high-speed trains (*trains à grande vitesse*—TGVs) and further expansion of the national network of limited access highways. French telecommunications are also among the world's best.

Roads: The French road network is the densest in the world and the longest in the European Union, with a total of about 985,000 kilometers of local, secondary, and main surfaced roads. This figure includes more than 10,000 kilometers of controlled-access divided highways, which gives France the second most extensive superhighway network in Europe. With a traffic density of 30 vehicles per kilometer, the French highway network is well below the European average of 44 vehicles per kilometer. This below-average traffic density facilitates the delivery of freight, 73 percent of which is carried by road in France.

Railroads: France's railroad system has a total of about 32,000 kilometers of track, including 167 kilometers of narrow (1 meter) gauge. Annual rail traffic in France comprises 315 million passengers on the main network, 560 million on the regional network around Paris, and 83 million on the high-speed train network. In 2003 the French rail system handled about 126 million metric tons of freight.

With its high-speed trains (*trains à grande vitesse*—TGVs), France holds the world land speed record—set in 2007—of 574.8 kilometers per hour. The TGVs, mainly passenger trains, run on about 1,500 kilometers of special track, traveling in normal commerical operation at 270 kilometers an hour. The TGVs connect cities in France, especially Paris, and in adjacent countries, including Belgium, Germany, and Switzerland. The first high-speed line opened in 1981 from Lyon to the outskirts of Paris. The TGV network grew through the 1990s, with extensions to Brussels, the introduction of the Eurostar service to London through the Channel Tunnel, and the extension of the TGV–Méditerranée track from Valence to Marseille, which entailed the construction of viaducts and extensive railroad cuttings. Opened in 2001, the latter extension reduced the travel time between Marseille and Paris to just three hours. For the sake of cost savings, much of the future development of high-speed services will involve the use of existing track and specially designed tilting trains.

In 1997, to promote greater efficiency across the French rail network, the French National Railroad Company which operates it, the Société Nationale des Chemins de Fer Français (SNCF), was reorganized, and the management of its track and related infrastructure was transferred to a new entity, the Réseau Ferré de France (RFF). When European Union–wide rail freight deregulation became effective in 2003, the RFF was obliged to open its track to freight operators other than the SNCF. Rail freight traffic as a proportion of France's total freight traffic has declined considerably over the past two decades, and this part of the SNCF's business has been operating at a loss.

Ports: Five of Europe's 15 busiest ports are located in France: the autonomous maritime ports (owned by the state) of Marseille, Le Havre, Dunkirk, St. Nazaire, and Bordeaux. These five ports, along with France's other autonomous ports of Rouen, Nantes, and Guadeloupe, control large port areas and handle 80 percent of the goods traffic through ports, more than 345 million metric tons of merchandise a year, half of all foreign trade. Some two dozen other ports, declared national ports for their significance, see 80 percent of all passenger port traffic.

Marseille is the largest French and Mediterranean port and the third largest in Europe in freight traffic, handling 95.5 million metric tons of cargo in 2002. Le Havre is France's largest container port and Europe's fifth ranked. Dunkirk, which handles 47.56 million metric tons annually, is growing in part because of cross-channel traffic. It is followed in tonnage by St. Nazaire, with 31.7 million metric tons, and Bordeaux, with 8.96 million metric tons.

French ports are international dispatching points with highly developed intermodal transport connections. The Compagnie Nouvelle de Conteneurs (CNC) ensures that sea freight from the main French ports is distributed daily throughout the country. The "Quality Net" European Network, with its hub in the French city of Metz, links the main French ports with surrounding European countries.

Inland Waterways: France has a system of large, navigable rivers, such as the Loire, Seine, and Rhône, that crisscross the country and, supplemented by connecting canals, have long been essential for trade and travel. The country has about 15,000 kilometers of waterways, 8,500 kilometers of which are heavily traveled. In 2001 the waterways transported more than 56 million metric tons of freight. The autonomous Port of Paris has become the leading river port in France and the second busiest in Europe, handling 20.3 million metric tons of merchandise. Le Havre, located on the Seine River estuary, is an important river as well as maritime port. Rouen is the largest port in Europe for grain export. Over the last few years, major operators of waterway transportation have worked to enhance its reliability and capacity to handle large volumes of cargo.

Civil Aviation and Airports: Because of its numerous urban and industrial centers, France has a particularly high number of airports. Of its 878 airports and airfields, 801 are paved, including 476 with runways more than 3,047 meters long. Three airports handle most of France's international passenger and cargo service, including Paris's two main airports, Orly to the south of Paris and Roissy–Charles de Gaulle to the northeast of Paris (with its own rail station on the high-speed train interconnection). The third international airport is Nice–Côte d'Azur. Other regional airports, notably Lyon's Saint-Exupéry (also with its own high-speed train station), have sought to expand their international services.

Through its international airports, France handles 6,200 flights every week. The two Paris airports handle 20 percent of the total airfreight in the European Union (EU). Their annual traffic growth of more than 10 percent greatly exceeds the 2 to 3 percent growth of most other European airports.

About 900 aircraft, including helicopters, operate under the French flag. The national carrier, Air France, was partly privatized in early 1999 and has recently operated in an environment of EU-wide deregulation. The location of the European Airbus project in Toulouse has turned the city into the European aviation center.

Pipelines: France's pipeline system carries crude oil over 3,059 kilometers of pipeline, petroleum products over 4,487 kilometers, and natural gas over 24,746 kilometers.

Telecommunications: The French telephone system, with some 39,200,000 telephones, is highly developed, relying for domestic traffic on extensive cable and microwave radio-relay networks, widely introduced fiber-optic systems, and satellite systems. The international system relies on two Intelsat earth stations (with a total of five antennas—two for the Indian Ocean and three for the Atlantic Ocean), high-frequency (HF) radio communications with more than 20 countries, Inmarsat service, and Eutelsat TV service.

Until 1997, the state-owned France Télécom had a monopoly on telecommunications in France. In 1997 the government began reducing its stake, now below 42 percent. While the partially privatized France Télécom maintains its monopoly on local calls, the telecommunications sector has been opened to competition in the European Union (EU)–wide deregulated market, and other companies offer telephone subscriptions for long-distance and medium-distance calls.

France Télécom, acquiring the British company Orange, secured its leading position in the highly competitive domestic mobile phone market. At the same time, acquisitions made France Télécom the world's most highly indebted company, requiring a rescue plan in late 2002. The financial future of the company as well as of the entire sector in France and EU-wide, is uncertain. Since the late 1990s, mobile phone subscriptions have risen sharply, but so has investment. At the end of 2001, 59.4 percent of the French population subscribed to a mobile phone service. Operating licenses for third-generation mobile phones, using Universal Mobile Telecommunications System (UMTS) technology, have been awarded to France Télécom, Cegetel, and Bouygues.

In Internet use, France is catching up to the world's leaders, after a slight lag. At the end of 2001, 31.9 percent of the French population—almost 19 million people—had Internet access, compared with 61.8 percent in the United States, 40.2 percent in the United Kingdom, and 37.7 percent in Germany. Among those with secondary education and above, the level is much higher. By late 2003, 93 percent of companies had Internet connections, and 56 percent had their own

Web sites. A few thousand French-owned online shopping sites exist, but French consumers have shown limited enthusiasm for e-commerce.

GOVERNMENT AND POLITICS

Political System Overview: The French Republic, known as the Fifth Republic, has a hybrid form of government with elements of both presidential and parliamentary systems. The French system features a prime minister and a president who are both active participants in the day-to-day functioning of government. The system differs from a typical parliamentary system in that it has a popularly elected president who is not a ceremonial figurehead, and it differs from a presidential system in that it has an executive prime minister who has some answerability to the legislature. France's current institutions are governed by the constitution of the Fifth Republic, which was approved by popular referendum in 1958. This constitution significantly strengthened the power of the executive authorities (the president and the government) and curtailed the authority of the legislature. Prior to 1958, France had a weak executive and suffered from government instability; during the Fourth Republic's 12-year existence, there were 26 different governments.

Executive Branch: Under the system forged by Charles de Gaulle, which remains largely in place, France has a strong, stable executive at the center of power. The French constitution gives executive authority to both the president and the prime minister. The president, who presides from the Elysée Palace, is the official head of state and commander in chief of the armed forces. The president is elected by direct universal suffrage to a five-year term of office, a term shortened by two years in 2002. The president is not term-limited. The prime minister, the head of government, is nominated by the National Assembly, the legislature's lower house, and appointed by the president. The prime minister leads the Council of Ministers or cabinet, whose members are not necessarily parliamentarians. The president appoints the cabinet on the recommendation of the prime minister. According to the power division that has evolved as a politcal convention, the president is mainly responsible for foreign policy and national defense and the prime minister for domestic policy. The governing process can be complicated in periods of so-called "cohabitation," in which the prime minister and president, who are elected separately, are from rival parties.

One of the president's most important powers is the right to dissolve the National Assembly and call new legislative elections. The president is also authorized to submit certain policy matters, e.g., European Union treaties, to national referenda. The prime minister retains significant authority as the leader of the majority party or coalition in the National Assembly. The balance of power between the president and prime minister depends on which party holds sway in the legislature. When the president has the strong support of a parliamentary majority, the prime minister tends to serve as a deputy of the president. When the president's party is in the minority, the president still appoints a prime minister from a party in the majority coalition. This results in a power-sharing arrangement—cohabitation—in which the president and prime minister tend to check each other's influence. The first episode of cohabitation occurred under Socialist president François Mitterrand, from 1986 to 1988, after the Socialist Party lost its majority in the National

Assembly. In 1997 President Jacques Chirac lost his conservative majority in the National Assembly, leading to a period of cohabitation with Socialist prime minister Lionel Jospin.

Legislative Branch: France has a bicameral legislature, with a National Assembly of 577 members and a Senate of 321 members (296 for metropolitan France, 13 for overseas departments and territories, and 12 for French nationals abroad). Under a 2003 law, to reflect demographic changes, the number of senators will increase to 346 by 2010.

Members (deputies) of the National Assembly, the principal legislative body, are directly elected to five-year terms in single-member electoral constituencies by a two-ballot system; all seats are voted on in each election. Senators, whose term was shortened from nine to six years in 2004, are elected indirectly through an electoral college consisting of elected officials in each department (roughly, state). The system introduces a rural, conservative bias in the composition of the Senate. However, the Senate's legislative powers are in practice limited. When the two houses of the legislature disagree, the final decision rests with the National Assembly.

Under the constitution of the Fifth Republic, the legislature's powers were reduced compared to those existing under the Fourth Republic. The agenda of the legislature is strongly influenced by the government, which can demand an up-or-down vote on legislation or even win its adoption without an actual vote. The president can dissolve the National Assembly before the end of its five-year term, as has happened five times since the inauguration of the Fifth Republic. At the same time, despite its diminished powers, the National Assembly can cause the government to fall if an absolute majority of the total Assembly membership votes to censure.

Judicial Branch: The most distinctive feature of the French judicial system is that it has two main branches, each with a hierarchy of appellate courts. One branch—the administrative order of courts—hears administrative cases (litigation involving disputes over government regulations or against public bodies). Another branch—the judicial or ordinary order of courts—hears civil and criminal cases.

Most cases involving administrative bodies or rules are heard initially by administrative tribunals. Appeals of decisions can move up through a series of courts, at the apex of which is the Council of State, a tribunal founded by Napoléon Bonaparte. The Council of State, which sits in the Palais Royal, is the final court of appeal on the legality of administrative acts or executive decisions. The council has the power to quash governmental decisions and regulations if they do not conform to applicable constitutional or statutory law, or to general principles of French law.

In the judicial or ordinary order of courts, the lower courts are of two main types, the civil courts and the criminal courts. The civil courts judge conflicts between persons or between persons and corporations. The criminal courts judge minor legal infractions (*contraventions*) and graver offenses (*délits*). Felonies are tried in assize courts (*cours d'assises*), the only courts with trial by jury. From the lower civil and criminal courts alike, appeals may be taken to appeals courts (*cours d'appel*), of which there were 27 in 2003. Judgments of the appeals courts and the assize courts are final, except that appeals on the interpretation of the law or points of procedure may be taken to the highest of the judicial courts, the Court of Cassation or the Supreme Court of Appeals in Paris.

Several specialized courts also exist. In the ordinary order of courts are, for example, commercial courts, industrial courts, and social security courts. In addition, there are high courts empowered to try crimes of a political nature by the president or misconduct by members of the government.

Administrative Divisions: Traditionally a strongly centralized state, France had two levels of subnational government dating back to the French Revolution, municipalities and departments. Each of the departments was headed by a prefect appointed by the central government. Since the mid-1980s, France has been decentralizing authority, creating a third, regional level of administration and providing for the first time for the direct election of regional councils. The three levels of administration now include 36,763 municipalities (*communes*), 100 departments, and 26 regions. The regions, which often roughly correspond to France's prerevolutionary provinces, group the departments and have jurisdiction over planning, development, vocational training and upper secondary educational institutions (lycées). The departments—96 in metropolitan France and four overseas (Martinique, Guadeloupe, Réunion, and French Guiana)—have authority over health care, social entitlements, and lower secondary education (*collèges*). Each department has both a prefect and an elected assembly. Each municipality has an elected council and a mayor. The mayor is elected locally but also represents the French state.

Judicial and Legal System: France has a system of civil law, which, in the tradition of coded Roman law, calls for applying statutes as written, rather than relying on case law and legal precedent. The legal system is a descendant of an extensive collection of laws drafted under the direction of Napoléon Bonaparte, the Code Napoléon. Current legislation must conform to the Constitution of the Fifth Republic of 1958 and to treaties, for example, the European Convention on Human Rights (accepted by treaty).

France's Constitutional Council, a new body established by the 1958 constitution, is the country's forum for constitutional review of legislation. Constitutional challenges may be raised to legislation during the period between its passage and promulgation (signature of the president). Such challenges may be brought by the president, the prime minister, the president of the Senate, the president of the National Assembly, 60 senators, or 60 deputies. Once promulgated, French legislation is not subject to judicial review. In recent years, challenges have been raised to aspects of France's antiterrorism legislation.

The core of the legal system is a body of civil servants, the magistrates. Trained and selected at the national school for magistrates, the magistrates are mainly of two groups, judges (and assisting lawyers) and prosecutors. Judges, although civil servants, enjoy special statutory protection from the executive. They may not be transferred without their consent. Their careers are overseen by the High Council of the Magistracy. Prosecutors, on the other hand, respond to the minister of justice in the executive branch. This organizational position of prosecutors regularly arouses the suspicion that they have been pressured to drop litigation against politicians suspected of corruption.

Legal tradition since the Napoléonic era has always given prosecutors strong powers. In 2004 the National Assembly passed a sweeping anticrime law that decreased the powers of judges and further augmented those of prosecutors, whose job is to convict, as well as the powers of the police. The controversial law's hundreds of revisions to the penal code enhanced police and prosecutorial powers to conduct surveillance and to detain and question suspects without charges and legal counsel. The exceptional powers for the police and prosecutors under the law are said to be aimed not at common crime but at organized criminal activities related to drug trafficking, terrorism, assassination, pimping, money laundering, illegal immigration, and torture. The new law has been seen as a political move on the part of the center-right to neutralize the far-right National Front party of Jean-Marie Le Pen, which takes a hard line on crime.

Notwithstanding the growing stringency of France's penal system and code, the death penalty, abolished in 1981, is not among the sentencing options that mainstream politicians contemplate.

Electoral System: Suffrage in France, extended to women in 1944, is now universal at age 18. The country has a two-round voting system for the National Assembly and president. Runoff elections are required if no candidate receives more than 50 percent of the vote in the first round. The most recent presidential election was held in April and May 2007. As no candidate obtained an absolute majority in the first round in April, a runoff round between the two leading candidates, Nicolas Sarkozy and Ségolène Royal, took place on Sunday, May 6. Presidential elections are followed in June by an election for deputies of the National Assembly.

As a requirement of European Union (EU) membership, the French parliament approved a constitutional amendment allowing citizens of EU member countries who are residents in France to vote in elections for seats on France's municipal councils. The same group may also vote to fill France's seats in the European Parliament, the representative assembly of the EU. Citizens of any EU country can be elected to a French municipal council or to a French seat in the European Parliament, but they may not serve as mayors.

Politics and Political Parties: For the past 25 years, France's government has alternated between two relatively stable party coalitions. On the left is a coalition led by the French Socialist Party (Parti Socialiste—PS) and including minor members such as the French Communist Party (Parti Communiste Français—PCF), The Greens (Les Verts), and the Left Radical Party (Parti Radical de Gauche—PRG). On the center-right is the current ruling coalition led by the Union for a Popular Movement (Union pour un Mouvement Populaire—UMP)—called Union for a Presidential Majority when first formed in 2002. The UMP was formed from a merger of the main center-right party, Rally for the Republic (Rassemblement pour la République—RPR), and a minor partner, the bulk of the Union for Democracy (Union pour la Démocratie Française—UDF), as well as the small Liberal Democracy (Démocratie Libérale—DL) party.

Other minor parties have some representatives, for example, Rally for France and the Independence of Europe (Rassemblement pour la France et l'Indépendance de l'Europe—RpFIE) and Citizen and Republican Movement (Mouvement Républicain et Citoyen—MRC). However, it is difficult for parties outside the major coalitions to make significant electoral inroads. Despite these difficulties, the far-right National Front (Front National—FN) has periodically had sizable successes in elections since 1983. In the mid-1980s, because the incentives of France's two-ballot electoral system favor inter-party alliances, the mainstream center-right parties flirted with a strategic alliance with the FN, but finally rejected it. Instead, the moderate right co-opted the FN's positions by taking a harder line on immigration and law and order.

Prominent figures of the center-right parties at present are President Nicolas Sarkozy, Prime Minister François Fillon, and several government ministers, Jean-Louis Borloo (economics), Alain Juppé (environment), and Michèle Alliot-Marie (interior), as well as Sarkozy's predecessor as president, Jacques Chirac, and Fillon's predecessor as prime minister, Dominique de Villepin. Prominent figures on the left are the Socialist Party's unsuccessful presidential candidate in the 2007 election, Ségolène Royal, who would have been France's first woman president, and François Hollande and Lionel Jospin, respectively, present and past heads of the Socialist Party.

Mass Media: French television is partly state-controlled and partly in private hands, with all television channels carrying advertising. Three channels—the flagship TF1, privatized in 1987, and the state-owned France 2 and France 3—typically account for about three-quarters of the total television audience. The growth of satellite and cable TV has led to a proliferation of channels, with the largest controlled by media giant Vivendi Universal. Other channels include the entertainment outlet Métropole 6 (M6), and the Franco-German channel, Arte, which broadcasts in both countries and languages. The international French-language channel TV5, co-financed by Belgium, Canada, and Switzerland, is available globally. French domestic TV channels have many viewers in Maghreb countries.

The leading radio outlets are RTL (Radio Télédiffusion Luxembourgoise) and Europe 1, both popular nationwide commercial stations, and France-Inter, the major French public radio network, and the all-news France Info, both part of Radio France. These radio outlets together account for more than one-third of the total radio audience. There are also numerous FM stations throughout the country. In addition, France's international broadcasters have significant audiences abroad. Radio France Internationale is one of the world's leading international stations—a kind of French World Service—with a widely heard Arabic-language offshoot, Radio Monte Carlo Moyen Orient.

France has more than 100 daily newspapers, most privately held and unaffiliated with political parties. The leading publications include the quality national daily newspapers, the highly regarded and best-selling *Le Monde*, with a center-left outlook (circulation 360,000); *Le Figaro*, with a right-of-center outlook (circulation 350,000); *Libération*, to the left of *Le Monde*; and *La Croix*. The two daily business newspapers are *Les Echos* (circulation 124,000 in 2001) and *La Tribune* (86,000). The sports daily, the famous *L'Equipe*, is also widely read (360,000 in 2001). The weekly news magazine with the largest circulation is *Paris-Match* (762,000 in 2000). Other major newsweeklies include *L'Express* and *Le Point*. France also has a strong regional daily press, the total circulation of which dwarfs that of the national press. The largest regional daily is *Ouest-France* in Rennes (773,000 in 2001). Another notable publication is the Paris-based *International Herald Tribune*, published in English.

Foreign Relations: Since World War II, France has played a leading international role, transforming itself from an major colonial power to the earliest and strongest advocate of European integration, as well as a strong supporter of broader international cooperation. France's most important bilateral tie since the 1960s has been with Germany. France views Franco-German cooperation, as well as the development of an independent European defense capability, as the keys to enhanced European security. In the mid-1990s, relations between Paris and Berlin became somewhat strained when German reunification altered the two countries' balance and Germany's leaders were less prepared than their predecessors to subordinate Germany's interests to French political leadership. Germany also sought to reduce its contributions to the European Union (EU) budget, a large share of which goes to subsidizing French agriculture. The two countries, leaving aside such frictions, took a common stand in opposing U.S.-led military action against Iraq in 2003.

France and the United States pursue parallel policies on most economic, political, and security issues and have a history of close cooperation, along with occasional strains. During the Cold War, tensions arose when France attempted to arbitrate between the United States and the Soviet Union. France also insisted on maintaining control of its nuclear arsenal, removing itself from the military leadership of the North Atlantic Treaty Organization in order to do so. Recent tensions arose in 2003 when France, unlike in the 1991 Gulf War, refused to back the use of force in Iraq. However, although France did not join the second U.S.-led coalition in Iraq, it joined the action in Afghanistan, contributed financially through the EU to Iraq reconstruction in 2003, and offered the Iraqi Interim Government assistance in the form of police training and debt relief. These actions have somewhat assuaged U.S. pique, as has the central role France has been playing in international efforts to combat terrorism. Some central figures in the Chirac administration, most notably, France's first female defense minister, Michèle Alliot-Marie, made improved Franco-American relations a priority since the Iraq War. The Sarkozy administration is expected to continue seeking improved relations.

In other regions of the world, France plays a significant role through commercial activities, extensive development assistance programs, and defense agreements. French influence is especially strong in francophone Africa and to a lesser extent in the Arab world. In the Middle East, France has been active in urging the establishment of a Palestinian state through a multilateral peace process and has provided significant assistance to the Palestinian Authority. France also has significant commercial and political relations in East Asia and Southeast Asia, as well as growing participation in regional organizations there. In Southeast Asia, France was an architect of the 1991 Paris Accords, which ended the conflict in Cambodia. In China, France is currently stepping up commercial competition with U.S. business. In Latin America, France has actively backed efforts to restore democracy to Haiti.

Membership in Major International Organizations: A charter member of the United Nations (UN), France has held one of the five permanent seats on the UN Security Council since 1945 and is a member of most of the UN's specialized and related agencies. France was a founding member of European Union (EU) in 1992 and of its several predecessor organizations, including the European Coal and Steel Community (ECSC), the European Economic Community (EEC), and the European Community (EC). France is a member of the North Atlantic Treaty Organization (NATO), the Organisation for Economic Co-operation and Development (OECD), the Organization for Security and Co-operation in Europe (OSCE), the World Trade Organization (WTO), the International Monetary Fund (IMF), the International Bank for Reconstruction and Development (IBRD) or World Bank, and the International Labor Organization (ILO). The country initiated the annual meetings of the seven leading industrial countries, the Group of Seven, now the Group of Eight with the addition of Russia, and has often held the top posts in the international organizations to which it belongs. In the first half of the

1990s, French nationals served simultaneously at the head of the European Commission, the IMF, the OECD, the European Bank for Reconstruction and Development (EBRD), and the secretariat of the Council of Europe (CE). In 2003 the presidency of the European Central Bank (ECB) also passed into French hands.

In addition to the main international organizations, France is a member of scores of others, including, to name a few categories, many organizations in regions where France was once a colonial power and organizations dedicated to cooperation in, for example, space, human rights, environmental protection, policing, and standard-setting for particular economic sectors. Placing a high priority on arms control and nonproliferation, France actively participates in the major supplier regimes that aim to restrict the transfer of essential technologies for weapons of mass destruction (WMD), e.g., the Nuclear Suppliers Group, the Australia Group (for chemical and biological weapons), and the Missile Technology Control Regime. France takes an active part in the Proliferation Security Initiative and is engaged with the United States, both bilaterally and at the International Atomic Energy Agency (IAEA) and the Organisation for the Prohibition of Chemical Weapons (OPCW), to curb WMD proliferation from North Korea, Iran, Libya, and elsewhere.

Major International Treaties: France is party to most of the major international treaties, accords, and conventions in many areas, for example, the environment, human rights, terrorism, and nuclear proliferation. The environmental agreements include global and regional accords on the atmosphere, hazardous substances, marine resources, and living resources of the sea, freshwater, and land. In the area of human rights, France has acceded to most of the significant international treaties, for example: Economic, Social and Cultural Rights; Civil and Political Rights; Discrimination against Women; Torture; and Rights of the Child. France is also a state party to some 11 terrorism-related conventions, including those on financing, bombing, plastic explosives, hostages, diplomatic agents, and the safety of air and maritime craft. France is a signatory to most accords on arms control and nuclear safety, for example, the Biological and Toxin Weapons Convention; the Chemical Weapons Convention; the Convention on the Prohibition of the Use, Stockpiling, Production and Transfer of Anti-Personnel Mines and on their Destruction; the Treaty on the Non-Proliferation of Nuclear Weapons; the Partial Test Ban Treaty; and the Comprehensive Test Ban Treaty. In the case of the last three treaties, France was slow to become a signatory. France signed the last in 1996 only after completing the final one of its 210 nuclear tests. France is a key player in the adaptation of the Treaty on Conventional Armed Forces in Europe to the new strategic environment.

NATIONAL SECURITY

Armed Forces Overview: Possessing an independent nuclear deterrent capability since the early 1960s, France is perhaps second only to the United Kingdom (UK) as West Europe's most powerful military force. France is also one of only three European countries, including the UK and Greece, that spend more that 2 percent of gross domestic product on the military. Like other Western countries in the aftermath of the Cold War, France has undertaken a major restructuring of its armed forces to develop a professional military that is smaller, more rapidly deployable, and better tailored for operations distant from France. Key elements of the restructuring included phasing out conscripts by 2002 in favor of an all-volunteer, technologically more intensive military force. In moving to a professional force, the French military was downsized by one-third between 1996 and 2002.

A total of 428,000 people work for the French Ministry of Defense (2005). This number includes 81,000 civilians and 347,000 military professionals in four main branches. The army comprises 39 percent (134,000 active military); the navy, 12 percent (43,000 active military); the air force, 17 percent (61,000 active military); and the Gendarmerie Nationale (a branch of the national police under military statute), 22 percent (about 100,000). The joint services and strategic nuclear forces make up another 10 percent. The reserves number about 100,000.

As France scales back and modernizes its force, it remains a key member of the Western system of alliances and institutions, and one of the largest contributors to the military capabilities of the North Atlantic Treaty Organization. France also remains the strongest advocate of a credible, independent European defense capability.

Despite its reduced size, the French military has participated in numerous United Nations–mandated peacekeeping operations, most notably, in former Yugoslavia, as well as in humanitarian relief operations in, for example, Darfur and tsunami-ravished parts of Asia. It also maintains garrisons and naval bases around the world, especially in sub-Saharan Africa.

Foreign Military Relations: In 1949 France was a founding member of the North Atlantic Treaty Organization (NATO), a regional defense alliance led by the trans-Atlantic partners. France has relied on NATO ever since, while also insisting on a degree of independence in military affairs. In 1966 France, wanting sole control of its nuclear weapons, withdrew its forces from NATO's integrated military command structure, while remaining a member of NATO's political councils. In 1995 France rejoined the military structure and has since worked actively to adapt NATO—internally and externally—to the post-Cold War environment. France is one of the major contributors to the NATO Reaction Force and, with about 4,000 troops, is the second largest member-state contributor to NATO operations, on a par with Italy and after Germany. Two French generals recently took command of the two major NATO forces, the International Security Assistance Force (ISAF) in Afghanistan and Kosovo Forces (KFOR).

France's involvement with NATO has not prevented French leaders from formulating plans to create an exclusively European integrated military force as a security supplement to relieve NATO from participating in some regional crises. France and the European Union (EU) in general do not currently have the capabilities necessary to create forces independent of NATO. However, France firmly backs strengthening the security arm of the EU and is a strong advocate of the 60,000-strong Rapid Reaction Force (RRF), to which France, Germany, and the United Kingdom (UK) are to be the major contributors. France also supports the Organization for Security and Co-operation in Europe (OSCE) and other efforts at cooperation. In order to advance the creation of a European defense identity, France seeks to enhance the coordination of the French defense industry within a European framework and to give a more European dimension to nuclear deterrence, still the cornerstone of French defense strategy. Working with other European countries, most notably Germany and the UK, France has long supported naval cooperation and agreed in 2004 to set up joint battle groups. Outside of NATO and Europe, France has numerous military agreements with former colonies, especially nations in Africa.

External Threat: Since the collapse of the Soviet Union and the creation and expansion of the European Union, France has little reason to expect any state-led form of military aggression against its mainland. France's main foreign intelligence service is the General Directorate for External Security (Direction Générale de la Sécurité Extérieure—DGSE).

Defense Budget: Among the larger European economies, France and the United Kingdom are the only significant spenders on defense. The two together account for 40 percent of European Union (EU) defense spending. Each spends well over 2 percent of gross domestic product (GDP), while most other EU countries spend less than 1.5 percent of GDP. In fiscal year 2007, France's defense budget is expected to reach US$45 billion, a modest dollar increase from 2006 that will represent 2.6 percent of GDP. A declining share of France's defense budget—now less than 10 percent—goes toward its nuclear force. For comparision with France's military expenditiures, the U.S. defense budget in 2007 will reach about 3.2 percent of GDP and dollar figures that dwarf the spending of the North Atlantic Treaty Organization (NATO) partners.

Major Military Units: As of 2006, France's army had 14 brigades, including two armored, two mechanized infantry, and two light armored, and one each of artillery, mountain infantry, airborne, air mobile, engineering, signal, international/electronic warfare, and French/German brigades. The army also includes regiments of the Foreign Legion, Marines, and Special Operations Forces. The navy, organized into commands, has the nuclear command, five territorial commands, and six organic commands for different kinds of ships. The navy also includes ground security and aviation units. The air force is divided into four commands: air signals and ground environment, air combat, air mobility, and air training.

Major Military Equipment: In 2006 the army had 926 main battle tanks; 1,809 reconnaissance vehicles; 601 armored infantry fighting vehicles; 4,413 armored personnel carriers; 787 artillery pieces; 1,195 antitank guided weapons; 455 air defense guns; 393 helicopters; and 68 unmanned aerial vehicles. The navy had six tactical and four nuclear submarines, one aircraft carrier (the nuclear-powered *Charles de Gaulle*), one helicopter carrier, 13 destroyers, 20 frigates, 36 patrol and coastal vessels, 21 mine warfare vessels, 10 amphibious vessels, and 23 support vessels. The navy also had 84 combat aircraft, including 30 armed helicopters. The air force had 478 combat aircraft, including 340 Mirage fighter aircraft; 28 helicopters; and four unmanned aerial vehicles.

France remains committed to the maintenance and continuous modernization of a relatively strong nuclear deterrent capability. In its strategic nuclear forces, France currently has roughly 350 nuclear warheads in two nuclear weapons systems, air-based and sea-based. The third, land-based system was removed from service after the Cold War-era threat from the Eastern Bloc dissolved. In the sea-based system, there are four nuclear-powered ballistic missile submarines (SSBNs) equipped with 64 submarine-launched ballistic missiles (SLBMs) with six warheads each. The air-based system consists of 60 Mirage 2000N and 28 Super Étendard aircraft equipped with a total of 60–90 medium-range air-to-surface missiles with single warheads. France intends eventually to replace all of its Mirage aircraft with the Rafale, its new multipurpose fighter-bomber, whose roles will include the delivery of both conventional and nuclear weapons. The Rafale program calls for 234 aircraft for the air force and 60 for the navy.

Military Service: Conscription, a feature of French life for more than a century, was phased out and finally ended in 2002, when France completed its move to all-professional armed forces. Despite the end of conscription, young people—both males and females—must still register for possible conscription. The age for voluntary military service is 17 years of age with parental consent or age 18. In 2005 males in the age cohort of 17 to 49 numbered 13,676,509, and those judged fit for military service numbered 11,262,661. Males who reached military age during 2005 numbered 389,204.

Paramilitary Forces: In addition to the regular armed forces, France maintains its paramilitary Gendarmerie Nationale, one of the police system's two branches. The gendarmerie is an integrated part of the national military organization and supported by the defense budget. The gendarmerie exercises police authority in rural and small urban areas, while the non-military branch of the police, the National Police, has jurisdiction over urban areas with more than 10,000 inhabitants. The gendarmerie, 101,399 strong, including 7,250 women, is the only part of the military that has recently increased in size. From 1990 to 2004, France's regular military forces lost nearly 43 percent of personnel, while the gendarmerie gained more than 13 percent. Increasing the relative weight of the gendarmerie in the overall array of the uniformed armed forces reflects the growing priority that the government places on the nation's internal security and, in particular, on combating terrorism. The paramilitary gendarmerie is the organization in France ultimately responsible for homeland security. Much of the increase in the military budget of 2003–8, an increase slated to reinforce the French military's capacity to fight terrorism, was devoted to bolstering the gendarmerie. The extra funds for the gendarmerie will be applied to renewing the vehicle fleet—with the replacement of 122 VBRGs (gendarmerie wheeled armored vehicles)—and additional surveillance, intervention, and rescue helicopters, as well as improved computer systems.

Military Forces Abroad: France has traditionally had a large military presence abroad. Currently, about 34,000 troops are assigned outside of metropolitan France. Somewhat more than half of these troops are deployed to meet prepositioning requirements, maintaining garrisons and naval bases around the world, notably in sub-Saharan Africa. France maintains permanent military bases in Chad, Côte d'Ivoire, Djibouti, Gabon, and Senegal. The remaining 13,000 to 16,000 troops deployed overseas take part—often in leading roles—in peacekeeping/coalition operations under international or defense agreements. As one of five permanent members of the United Nations (UN) Security Council, France is a frequent volunteer for peacekeeping operations. French troops participate as part of the North Atlantic Treaty Organization (NATO) or of coalitions in stabilization efforts mandated by UN resolutions, or, on occasion, operate under the Eurocorps flag. Such actions are currently taking place in Africa, the Balkans, Afghanistan, and the Middle East, with some addressing humanitarian crises, such as in Darfur. To address crises, France deployed military forces to Côte d'Ivoire in 2002, to the Central African Republic in 2003, and, with European Union (EU) partners, to the Democratic Republic of the Congo in 2003. In 2004 it deployed military forces to monitor the Chad–Sudan border.

The French have been among the strongest supporters of NATO and EU policy in the Balkans. France is the largest contributor of troops in Kosovo, with 2,380 troops, or almost 14 percent of Kosovo Forces (KFOR). France has been the second largest partner of the United States in Afghanistan after Germany. French contributions include its *Charles de Gaulle* carrier battle group and 1,800 troops.

Despite foreign policy disagreements over Iraq, France and the United States remain strong partners in advancing security throughout the world. For example, 10,000 French forces in the Indian Ocean and the Pacific monitor sea-lanes. In another example, 7,000 French troops in the Caribbean area and French Guiana work closely with the U.S. Joint Interagency Task Force South to counter drug trafficking. France is also a full partner in the U.S.-initiated Proliferation Security Initiative and offers numerous training exercises.

Police: France is one of the most policed states in the world, with approximately 394 public personnel per 100,000 inhabitants. The French system of policing, like many others in Europe, differs significantly from that of the United States, which features city police departments. The French police are a national force led by chiefs in Paris. In the provinces, police forces answer not to mayors but to the regional administrators known as prefects. The policing system is composed of two separate organizations, the civilian National Police and the military gendarmerie, as well as one further component, the Directorate of Territorial Security (Direction de la Surveillance du Territoire—DST). The minister of interior controls the National Police and the DST and exercises operational control over the gendarmerie.

The National Police, with its 180,000 employees, operates mostly in large cities and towns as a general-purpose police force. It conducts security operations, such as patrols and traffic control, and, under the supervision of the judiciary, its "judiciary police" carries out criminal inquiries. The gendarmerie, when operating in civil contexts, conducts general policing in rural areas.

The intelligence arm of the police, the DST, which has no real U.S. equivalent, descended from the political police of Napoléonic times. Once engaged in spying on leftists and other suspect groups, it now conducts election analysis, monitors hooligans and casinos, and, most importantly, collects information on the interconnected threats of Islamist extremism and organized crime.

France's anticrime law, passed in 2002, increases police numbers and expands police powers, lowering thresholds for stop-and-search and for recording personal information in law enforcement databases. The law, although billed as aimed against serious crime, such as terrorism and organized crime, construes the latter broadly enough to include petty offenses such as begging.

Internal Threat: France's current concerns about domestic security —a central theme of elections in 2002—focus mainly on common crime and antisocial behavior, organized crime, and terrorism, especially Islamist terrorism. Since late 2005, the prospect of urban unrest also has become a matter of concern. At that time, widespread rioting erupted in France's city outskirts and reached a scale not seen in France since the student-worker riots of 1968. In the several weeks of rioting in 2005, the children of mainly North African immigrants burned some 10,000 cars and community centers and schools in 300 urban areas—areas where unemployment is rampant among young males. The property destruction was extensive and led to nearly 3,000 arrests and an official state of emergency lasting until January 2006. These riots aroused more consternation than the usual politically charged actions arising out of France's tradition of wildcat strikes, street demonstrations, and mass mobilization. Many interpreted the 2005 riots as evidence of the failure of French policies on immigration and integration, particularly of Muslims. A few even saw the riots as fueled by religion and hostile teachings in mosques. Others dismissed any causal connection to religion, blaming the mayhem simply on small numbers of gang leaders competing in destruction and exploiting the social disaffection of other underclass youth. Whatever the interpretation, the riots ensured that law and order and immigration were major themes in the electoral campaigns of 2007, recalling the dominance of security concerns in the 2002 presidential election, when the far-right leader Jean-Marie Le Pen polled a startling 17 percent in the first round of voting. In 2007 Nicolas Sarkozy, a relative hard-liner on law and order and immigration, garnered votes previously given to Le Pen, whose vote total fell to 10 percent.

Another of France's security concerns, crime, includes both ordinary crime and organized crime. The rate of common crime in France is about on a par with Europe's generally low rates. However, the perception is widespread that crime is increasing, perhaps because, in urban areas, the level of reported crime involving guns is rising. A disproportionate share of common crime is committed by minority youths—Muslim and black—who make up half of the prison population. Organized crime also continues to plague France's Mediterranean coast, with hotspots in Nice and Marseille for drug trafficking, robbery, and prostitution. Criminal activities, especially by organized groups, in turn have linkages with another major security concern, terrorism. Criminal activities such as the trafficking of drugs, weapons, and women and various forms of financial crime are sources of funding for radical Islamist groups.

France's response to its security concerns has involved significant recent reforms in both its immigration and integration policies and in its legal regime and law enforcement apparatus. France continues to tighten its requirements for entry, stay, and naturalization in the country, while at the same time stepping up affirmative action for the underprivileged section of its population. In 2004 France passed a bill that makes it possible to deport non-citizens for inciting "discrimination, hatred, or violence" against any group. This law has been used to deport radical Muslim clerics. The country has also increased the already strong powers of the police and prosecutors under the law and reinforced the capabilities and interoperability of its intelligence agencies and counterterrorism units.

Terrorism: France's concern with countering terrorism is of long standing. Since 1980, terrorist acts have been perpetrated on French soil by three types of groups, French radical leftists, European regional separatists (i.e., Corsican and Basque nationalists), and internationally linked Muslim militants. The radical leftists, never as threatening as similar groups in Germany and Italy, ceased to pose a problem by the late 1980s. Separatist terrorism made its latest major showing in the 1998 assassination of the highest French government official in Corsica and continues in small-scale attacks on vacation homes there. At present, international terrorism, specifically Middle Eastern and Muslim fundamentalist terrorism, remains the chief concern.

Over the course of the 1980s, France became the European country most affected by such international terrorism, with a dozen bombings in 1986 by Palestinian groups demanding the release of political prisoners. Since the 1990s, the international terrorist threat has evolved into a religious extremist threat. France became the target of radical Islamist networks linked with Algeria's internal conflict and the most notorious Algerian terror faction, the Armed Islamic Group (Groupe Islamique Armé—GIA), part of Osama Bin Laden's Afghanistan-based network. These Algerian Islamists attacked France for supporting the military-backed Algerian government, which abrogated the Islamists' 1992 electoral victory in Algeria. Between 1993 and 1996, the GIA network assassinated 42 French expatriates (including Christian religious figures) in Algeria. In 1994 the GIA hijacked an Air France flight in Algiers with plans to crash it into the Eiffel Tower. In 1995 and 1996, the network detonated 10 bombs in public places.

In response to such threats, the French government has developed perhaps the strictest counterterrorism system in Europe, with antiterrorism laws that support preemptive arrests and an efficient intelligence apparatus that aggressively gathers and pools information on suspicious people and activities. Through this apparatus, France has played a central role in the world's antiterrorism efforts since September 11, 2001.

France has three main services responsible for investigating terrorist threats, the Directorate of Territorial Security (Direction de la Surveillance du Territoire—DST), under the Interior Ministry; the Central Directorate of General Information (Direction Centrale des Renseignements Généraux—DCRG or RG); and the National Antiterrorist Division (Division Nationale Antiterroriste—DNAT). The DST, formed in 1944 to counter espionage and political threats, is now the central security agency charged with countering the interconnected threats of organized crime and Islamist terrorism. Since 1995, the DST has deployed extensive wiretaps and used various human intelligence-gathering methods—some controversial—to keep informed of threats. The DST and the other intelligence services have built a large network of perhaps 10,000 informants throughout Muslim communities in France and abroad. The informants may receive money and legal favors, such as immigration papers and reduced prison sentences, in exchange for information about, for example, hate speech in mosques. The intelligence services feed a massive database of suspects or "persons of interest," whose movements, acquaintances, and trips abroad are monitored. In an effort to quantify the threat that France faces, the DCRG developed a formula, as follows: in a given Muslim population in Europe, an average of 5 percent are fundamentalists, and up to 3 percent of those fundamentalists should be considered dangerous. By that calculation, France's Muslim population of 6 million includes 300,000 fundamentalists, 9,000 of whom are potentially dangerous.

Through the data collection and clandestine monitoring of its various intelligence services, France has uncovered and dismantled Islamist networks on its soil, such as several groups that recruited terrorists for Iraq. From 2000 to 2005, the DST has been credited with thwarting terrorist acts in various stages of planning, with the arrests of several hundred involved militants. Thwarted plots included planned attacks on the U.S. Embassy in Paris, on French tourist sites on Réunion in the Indian Ocean, and on other targets. Following the 2005 bombings in London, French officials worked closely with their British counterparts. They have also regularly aided counterterrorism investigators in other countries, including the United States. France also plays an active role in the United Nations Security Council's Counterterrorism Committee and the Group of Eight's Counterterrorism Action Group.

Human Rights: The main human rights issues that currently arouse concern in France stem from the legal, judicial, and intelligence reforms that target terrorism. France's antiterrorism regime now supports constant operational surveillance of Islamic groups, defines the intent to commit terrorism as already a crime, provides wide scope to decide what constitutes terrorism, sets a low threshold for preemptive arrests and detentions without prompt counsel, and provides for wide latitude in judicial decision making. The entire system for monitoring and pursuing terrorists arguably outstrips the systems of most other democratic societies, including the United States, in both the system's effectiveness and invasiveness.

Human rights groups, such as the Human Rights League, as well as large numbers of France's defense magistrates have raised concern about French antiterrorism laws, charging an erosion of civil rights in the name of fighting terrorism. According to such critics, the legislation that makes "conspiracy to commit terrorism" a crime opens the door to arbitrary enforcement because a number of acts, which are not otherwise illegal, become illegal when a magistrate decides they occur in the context of intent to commit terrorism. Critics also charge that antiterrorist magistrates have excessive scope to decide what constitutes terrorism or the intent to commit it.

Another prominent human rights concern in recent years centers on the French government's 2004 ban on the wearing of "conspicuous religious symbols" in public schools. The law, whose primary target is the wearing of Muslim headscarves in school, is viewed by many in France and abroad as incompatible with the principle of freedom of religion. The law is also criticized as an official manifestation of anti-Islamic prejudice.